MW01128025

Everything You Need to Know

WHEN A PARENT DOESN'T SPEAK ENGLISH

People from all over the world immigrate to English-speaking
countries and become citizens.

• THE NEED TO KNOW LIBRARY •

Everything You Need to Know

WHEN A
PARENT DOESN'T
SPEAK ENGLISH

Patricia Lakin

THE ROSEN PUBLISHING GROUP, INC.
NEW YORK

Published in 1994 by The Rosen Publishing Group, Inc.
29 East 21st Street, New York, NY 10010

First Edition
Copyright 1994 by The Rosen Publishing Group, Inc.

Manufactured in the United States of America.

Library of Congress Cataloging-in-Publication Data

Lakin, Pat.
    Everything you need to know when a parent doesn't speak English
/ Patricia Lakin. — 1st ed.
        p.   cm.
    Includes bibliographical references and index.
    ISBN 0-8239-1691-X
    1. Children of immigrants—United States—Juvenile literature.
2. Children of immigrants—Education—United States—Juvenile
literature. 3. Americanization—Juvenile literature. 4. Acculturation—
United States—Juvenile literature. [1. Immigrants—United States.
2. United States—Emigration and immigration. 3. Parent and child.
4. English language—Study and teaching—Foreign speakers.] I. Title.
HQ796.L244 1994
303.48'2—dc20   94-1905
                                                                   CIP
                                                                    AC

Contents

Introduction

Do you have a parent who does not speak English? One of the most common reasons in America or other English-speaking countries for a person not to know English is because that person was born somewhere else. Your parents and even you may be *immigrants*. Immigrants are people who were born in one country but left there to make a permanent home in another country.

If your parents left their native country because they were no longer safe there, then your family are *refugees*. Refugees are people who live in another country until their real home becomes safe enough for them to return. Or perhaps your family has relocated for a set number of years because one of your parents has taken a new job.

All people who leave their homeland face many adjustments and new experiences. The language in their new home may not be the same language they first learned as a child. The first language you learn is called your *native language.* Your parent probably knows his or her native language but may not know English.

Whatever the reasons for moving, you and your parents now live in an English-speaking country. This is your home—for good or for a while. And having a parent who does not speak English may make you feel different from many of your friends or classmates. It also means that you may have certain jobs and responsibilities at home that your friends don't have. There may be times that you have to speak, read, or write for your non-English-speaking parent.

This book discusses what it feels like to have a parent who does not speak English. It gives some reasons why a parent may not have learned the language even though he or she may have lived in a new country for quite some time. It also explains why learning a language may be very difficult for your parent. And it shows you some practical ways to help your parent if he or she wants to learn English now.

Someday, you may come to understand and appreciate your parents and your heritage more fully. Having a different ethnic background from neighbors or friends isn't always easy, but far from being a source of shame, it can be something to celebrate.

Many foreign-speaking people make their home in large cities.

Chapter 1

You Are Not Alone

Since America first became a country over 200 years ago, more than 50 million American citizens were born in another land.

America is considered a nation of immigrants. During the 1980s, the number of U.S. residents who considered English to be a foreign language rose to 31.8 million people. This was due largely to a wave of immigration from Latin America, Asia, and Europe. Australia had heavy immigration from Europe after World War II. More recently, Asians, particularly the Vietnamese, have made their homes in "multicultural" Australia.

Canada, too, is composed of many ethnic communities. Since 1984, there has been a heavy influx of Chinese immigrants from Hong Kong,

9

over 10,000 of whom have become Canadian citizens. Unlike the "melting pot" of the United States, Canada's immigrant groups still tend to stay together and remain somewhat separate.

All things considered, your family is not as different as you may think. There are many people, especially in the larger cities, who have a good idea of what it's like to be in a new country. And like you, they may have a family member who does not speak English. So when you are at school, riding a bus, or in a crowd of people, stop and look around; you are not as alone as you may think.

Mixed Feelings

Even though you may be new to this country, you will meet lots of children your age at school. Through them you get to see up close what children born here are like. You may want to "fit in" and be accepted by them. As you try to fit in with a new group, you may develop some confusing feelings about your family. More and more, you may feel embarrassed by your family's different customs, foods, traditions, and language. You may think that you need to change your family's lifestyle in order for you to feel more "American" or "Canadian" or "Australian."

You may also begin to resent the extra demands made on you because you have a parent who can't speak English. Unlike your friends, you may be expected to act more grown-up. You may play an important part in family discussions and decisions. While your friends enjoy leisure time and are allowed to be carefree, you are not. You may have every minute of your day planned for you.

And if you're from a very small family or one of the only immigrant families in town, you may feel even more confused and unhappy.

Throughout this book, you will read about young people who are immigrants. All of them have at least one non-English-speaking parent. As you read their stories, imagine how they are feeling. It may help you to think more clearly and more positively about your own family situation.

Tanya's Story

My name is Tanya. My family comes from Kiev, Ukraine. We tried over and over to get to America. In America, my father would tell us, "there is a chance to get a good education." "And no long lines of people just to get a loaf of bread," my mother adds.

So finally, we got all of the papers in order and we had the money for our trip. We have lived in Brooklyn, New York, for three years, now. I am 14 years old but I am in a classroom with younger children. It is because of my English. I can talk and understand, but the reading is hard for me.

I hear the other children talk. Some of them say that their parents give them a little help with the homework. For me, that is impossible. My father works from morning until very late at night. He is a painter. Well, he wasn't always a painter. He was an engineer. But he must take a test in English and he needs to study. So he has no time for me. And my mother does not speak English at all. She tells me our alphabet letters look very different. When I show her one of my school books, she looks at the letters and throws up her hands. "Such a mystery, this English," she says in Russian.

Kim's Story

My name is Kim and I am 12. I was born in Pusan, South Korea. I am the youngest boy. I have an older sister and brother. My whole family came to live in America six years ago. My mother and father thought that America would offer us more opportunities. My older brother and sister and I love to study music. We are also good students and enjoy learning many new things.

Because I came here at such a young age, I am able to speak English quite well. My older sister and brother also speak English as if they were born here. My mother speaks with a heavy accent. But my father does not speak any English at all. I think that he probably understands a little, but I am not sure. He says people here speak so fast that it is difficult for him to figure out what they say. He refuses even to try to learn the language. My father is a very proud man. Perhaps he is nervous that he will appear foolish. I feel bad for my father, but I do not know how to help him.

Children often work in family-owned businesses where parents may not speak English.

Hwong's Story

My name is Hwong. I am the oldest of four children. I came to Canada four years ago when I was nine. I do not remember too much of our life before, and my parents will not answer my questions. I only know that things were very bad in Kampuchea (Cambodia). My family had to leave Kampuchea to save our lives. We are not really immigrants, they say. We are refugees. We were brought to Canada by some very kind people who gave us an apartment to live in. If things get better in our country, however, we will go back to live in Kampuchea. The thought of leaving Canada makes me sad. I have many friends here now. This is not so for my parents. My father must work all day and half the night. He washes dishes in different restaurants. My mother stays at home and dreams of her life in Kampuchea. She is very lonesome. And she hates the cold Canadian winters and all the snow. I wish that she could make friends like me. If only my mother would leave the house and learn English, maybe then she would begin to like her new home. She does not understand what this country has to offer.

Juan's Story

I am Juan Martinez and I have a very big family. We came from Mexico about five years ago. My relatives live close to us in a small midwestern town. Just last week my whole family had a big fiesta. We celebrated two things—our coming to the United

States and my eleventh birthday. There was plenty of good food. I got lots of presents and there was my favorite candy in the piñata.

I wish some of my school friends could have seen the piñata and tasted my mother's cooking. But I am different at school. My teacher calls me John. I play baseball and basketball with my classmates, but my friends know nothing about my family or that my mamma can't speak English. Sometimes it can get pretty confusing. But I tell myself not to worry. I can have fun at home, being Juan, and have fun at school, being John.

Chapter 2

What's It Like?

Did you know that you may have something in common with former statesman Henry Kissinger, New York's Governor Mario Cuomo, former presidential candidate Michael Dukakis, singer Gloria Estefan, actor Raul Julia, newscaster Connie Chung, and sports figures Nancy Lopez and Patrick Ewing? All these accomplished people were either immigrants themselves or the children of immigrants. That means it is very likely that one or both of their parents came to America not speaking English.

These well-known people seem to have made their way in the world. But can you imagine what their lives were like before they became famous? They probably felt many of the same pressures and

Many famous persons (like Gloria Estefan, above) are the children
of immigrants.

frustrations that you experience living with a parent who does not speak English. They probably had to: translate for their parents; shop for the family; help siblings with schoolwork; be responsible for getting places on their own; and maybe even work to support the family. Life for them, and maybe for you now, could be rather complex and demanding.

Juan's Worlds Collide

Juan thought he could separate his family life from his school life. One day, his school sent home a notice to all the parents and students in Juan's grade. It was an invitation to come and hear the principal speak about the junior high school program. Juan's father read the letter and was pleased. Both he and his wife were interested in their son's education.

Unfortunately, Juan's father was ill on the night of the meeting. Juan was nervous as he and his mother walked into his school without his father. Juan knew his mother did not understand very much English. Now his friends and teachers would know it, too.

When school friends talked to his mother, Juan hoped that she would pretend to understand. But instead, she asked her son to translate their conversation. Juan was embarrassed. It got worse as the evening continued. Juan had to listen closely to understand and remember what the principal was saying, then repeat everything to his mother in her language. Even though Juan spoke to his mother as quietly as he could, a woman sitting in front of them turned around and gave Juan an unfriendly look. She said he was "a rude boy."

Juan was getting angry. "I wish my father were here," Juan thought. "I hate to go anywhere with just my mother." Juan didn't care about next year's classes that night, he just wanted to go home.

Hwong Tries Her Best

Hwong's teacher noticed that something was wrong and asked to see Hwong after school. Hwong explained that she was getting worried about her mother. After school, she would find her mother asleep or crying. And when her mother spoke in her native language, Hwong didn't always understand right away because Hwong was in the habit of using English. This upset her mother even more.

Hwong's teacher had an idea. She told Hwong that the school needed to hire several more people to work afternoons in the cafeteria. It was a job that Hwong's mother could learn easily. It was also an opportunity for her mother to get out of the house, make new friends, and maybe start to learn some English, too. Hwong was delighted. For a long time, she had wanted her mother to know more about her life at school and her friends.

Hwong's mother was not as enthusiastic about the job as her daughter. It took days of begging for Hwong even to get her to come to school for an interview. As they sat in the principal's office together,

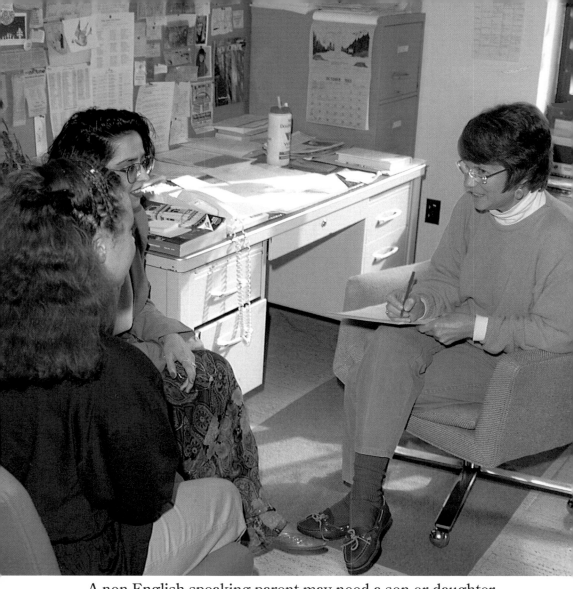

A non-English-speaking parent may need a son or daughter to translate during a job interview.

Hwong felt very grown-up. She translated for her mother, and everything seemed to be going well. Hwong was a little nervous when the principal handed her mother an application to fill out. Hwong wasn't sure what to do with items like "social security number," "previous work experience," and "refer-ences." Thinking fast, Hwong asked if they could fill out the form at home. They thanked the principal for his time and said they would contact him by the end of the week.

Hwong wasted no time. The next day she went to the library. The woman behind the desk was very helpful. She showed Hwong two shelves filled with books to help families like hers. There was practical information about using English in daily life, laws and civil rights, and how to become a citizen. Some books were all about business and finding a job, filling out forms, and writing a business letter. After hours of reading, Hwong was able to fill out most of the questions on her mother's application. But Hwong still needed help with the social security number. She asked her teacher the next day about it. Hwong's teacher volunteered to take Hwong and her mother downtown to the Social Security office and apply for a number.

Hwong's mother had the job if she wanted it. A final interview was set up with the principal to go over the paperwork and plan a work schedule. Hwong was proud of her own efforts and grateful to her teacher. Everything seemed fine, but not for long.

Hwong's mother refused to return for the second interview. Hwong had to face the principal and her teacher alone. She tried to explain to them why her mother was not accepting the job, but Hwong did not truly understand it herself. She was upset with her mother for a long time. And she felt even more frustrated and hopeless than before.

Showing Signs of Stress

Like Juan and Hwong, there may be times when you have mixed feelings about your family. This does not mean that you don't love them or care about them. It means that you are feeling and reacting to different emotions at the same time. And some of these emotions may be uncomfortable. For example, on one hand, you may feel obligated and responsible for your parents who have the disadvantage of not speaking English. On the other hand, you may feel resentful and angry about the added responsibility put on you for their well-being.

When a flood of emotions is stirred up inside a person, it's something like a volcano. You may want to "erupt" by walking out or yelling. But you don't usually behave this way, and you know your family would not understand or approve. Yet feelings like anger, frustration, disappointment, blame, confusion, or guilt don't just go away. What do you do? How do you cope? Since you don't see an acceptable way to "let off some steam," the pressure builds. This pressure and mental strain is called *stress*.

Everyone has some stress in life, especially during the teenage years. Teens are trying to discover who they are and who they want to be while their bodies are going through rapid change. A reasonable amount of stress is not necessarily bad. For some people stress is manageable, maybe even necessary. It gets them to focus on what needs to be done—a helpful mental push. And some people can withstand more stress than others before it becomes harmful. You must learn to recognize the warning signs of stress overload. When have *you* reached your limit? At what point do *you* lose control?

Look over the following list. Does it describe the way you have been feeling lately?

- Irritable, short-tempered
- Jittery, excitable, can't relax
- Tired
- Shy, withdrawn, quieter than usual
- Upset stomach, headache, heart beating faster
- Making a big deal over little things

It is always best to talk about your feelings. You may be better able to control your feelings when you can properly identify them and understand where they come from. You may want to sort things out with the help of a friend, family member, teacher, religious adviser, or professional counselor. You may want to read the life stories of some of the more famous immigrant children and see how they got through the difficult times. The important thing is not to keep bad feelings inside. Chances are that you will see things more clearly if you give yourself time to explore your feelings. You may come up with new ways to cope with those things in your life that you cannot change.

Children of immigrants often are the first members in the family to learn English.

Chapter 3

Why Your Parent(s) May Not Speak English

There are many reasons why a person can live in an English-speaking country and not learn to speak the language. The most common reasons are:

- lack of opportunity
- lack of necessity
- lack of desire
- lack of confidence.

None of the reasons given imply that the person is dumb or lazy.

Your Own Experience

Think about your own experience. When you came to this country, chances are that you went to school almost immediately. In school, you heard

English spoken for six hours a day. You may even have been given special classes to help you learn English more quickly. During the school day, you also saw lots of books, bulletin boards, and signs that were written in English. Even though you might not have been able to read them right away, you were getting to know what the letters looked like. You met new people and were anxious to make friends with English-speaking kids. As they tried to communicate with you, your knowledge of English grew.

You did your homework in English, too, which also helped you to improve your language skills. And later in the evening you may have listened to the radio, watched television, or spoken to a classmate on the phone. Again, you were exposed to English in normal, everyday situations. Your parents' experience, however, may have been quite different. They still may not be able or willing to overcome their past disadvantages.

Kim's Dad

Kim's dad asked him to wait outside while he went into the hardware store. After 15 minutes had passed, Kim went inside to see what was taking him so long. All he needed to buy were some simple tools. Kim saw his dad standing at the counter. He was looking sad and embarrassed. It was clear what had taken so long. He tried asking the clerk for what he needed, but he couldn't pronounce the words properly.

Watching TV may be a good way for an adult to practice English.

The clerk kept shaking his head saying, "I can't understand you, mister."

Kim rushed back outside without being noticed. He didn't want his dad to know he had seen what had happened. His dad was a proud man and wouldn't ask Kim for help. This kind of thing had happened before. Kim's dad had gotten discouraged and refused to speak English for a long time. Kim hoped that somehow his dad could make himself understood this time. It could give him the confidence he needed to keep trying.

Kim remembered the time in school when he thought the word for "pen" was "pan." A boy named Sam smiled and corrected him. They later became friends. Sam turned Kim's mistake into a joke. Sam's nickname for Kim is "Pan." And that's just fine with Kim. "If only my dad could put his pride aside," Kim wished, "maybe he would learn something by his language mistakes."

Tanya's Mom

My father and I have figured out why my mother has not learned any English. She doesn't have to! In the neighborhood where we live, there are many other immigrants. Russian is spoken more often in the area than English. My mother can shop, go to the bank, visit a doctor, and do everything she needs to do and still speak Russian. If there is something written that she does not understand, there are plenty of people around her to translate.

Things are different for my father and me. My father says if he did not know some English, he could not work as a painter and we would not have money to buy food and pay the rent. If I did not learn English, I would fail in school. When I first started school here three years ago, my teacher kept telling me, "Speak English, Tanya." I had no choice but to speak English all day long. I used to get a big headache trying to speak a new language. But now I am glad. I know two languages very well—Russian and English. I can travel, read signs, and make friends anywhere. I do not have to stay only in my neighborhood to be understood.

Get the Facts

If you don't already know the history of your family's immigration, ask your parents. Tell them you would like to know what life was like for them. Did they come willingly to their new home? Did they come with other relatives or by themselves? How old were they when they arrived? Did they move into a neighborhood where their native language was spoken?

Ask your parents directly why they haven't learned to speak English. Ask them if they wish to learn it now. If the answer is no, you must respect their wishes even if you disagree with them. A better understanding, however, of your parents' resistance to learning English may help you to accept their decision.

Parents and children can work together to learn English.

Chapter 4

Take Another Look

It's important to take a positive look at your non-English-speaking parent(s). Remember, his or her inability to speak English is not just a problem for you. It can be a problem for your parent(s). And one that may not go away. But it should not cloud your feelings for your parent. No one (including a parent) should be judged only by the language he or she chooses to speak.

There are many things to appreciate about your non-English-speaking parent. Think about what he or she *has* accomplished. Ask your parent questions about your family and your culture. You may learn some interesting things that you did not know before.

Photos of family members may reinforce feelings of pride in ethnic traditions.

Did you ever hear the description, the "immigrant personality"? It is a positive *trait*. A trait is a recognized quality. And this trait means that your immigrant parents had the physical and mental strength to leave their native land. They also had to be clever and resourceful to get to their new home. And, once here, they had to show determination to carry out their plan of making a new life for themselves and their family. All of these accomplishments are to be admired.

Hidden Treasures

Juan started asking his mother about her life as a young girl in Mexico. Her eyes lit up as she talked about her joy at winning the town's art competition. Her painting of the Mexican hero Miguel Hidalgo y Costilla was displayed in the town square. Juan had never known his mother could paint.

"Where is the painting?" he asked her. She led him up to the attic, where she had carefully wrapped her work in newspaper. Juan was impressed by his mother's talent and curious about her choice of subject. His mother promised to read him a book, in Spanish, about several important Mexicans.

Juan asked his mother why she didn't learn any English even though they had lived in America a long time. She admitted that she felt learning at her age was too difficult. Juan made a deal with his mother. If she would teach him about his Mexican heritage, he would try to help her learn English.

A Courageous Past

After being so disappointed and upset with her mother for not taking the job at school, Hwong decided to speak with her father. Hwong wanted to understand her mother—maybe her father could help. Hwong asked her father some questions about life in Kampuchea. Her father told her about his wife's courage and later despair. They had both left many relatives behind. The family was against the government that took over in Kampuchea. Hwong's mother hid some of the young men who were also against the new government. She saw much torture and death. He also told Hwong that when they first met, Hwong's mother was a happy young woman who loved to work in her vegetable garden.

"We are planning a spring garden at school!" shouted Hwong. Suddenly, many thoughts and ideas rushed into her head. Maybe she had been too quick to judge her mother. Hwong was determined to try to help her mother again.

Your Parents' Native Language

In trying to be like other English-speaking children, perhaps you have lost an appreciation of your native language. When you and your parents speak the words of that language, listen with extra care. Are there some characteristics of the language that you like better than English? Are there words and expressions that really describe feelings or situations better?

Writer and lecturer Richard Rodriguez remembers his childhood in his book *Hunger of Memory*. He writes:

> A family member would say something to me [in Spanish] and I would feel myself specially recognized. My parents would say something to me [in Spanish] and I would feel embraced by the sounds of their words. Those sounds said: 'I am speaking with ease in Spanish. I am addressing you in words I never use with *los gringos* [the Americans]. I recognize you as someone special, close, like no one outside. You belong with us. In the family.'

Rodriguez talks about English as the language spoken outside his family— the "public" language. Eventually, Rodriguez became a professor of English Literature. But his early memories of the Spanish language are still with him.

Know What You're About

In Janet Bode's book *New Kids on the Block*, a Mexican boy discusses his use of English and Spanish in the home.

> My dad doesn't speak Spanish that well but he understands everything. And even though my mother doesn't speak English, she understands it. When my father and mother talk, she speaks to him in Spanish and he answers her in English. I talk to my dad in English and my mother in Spanish. I'm used to it; it's what I've always known. What matters is that I know what I'm about and so do the important people in my life.
> I don't understand kids who are angry at their parents and their culture. You are what you are.

Close family ties have helped many immigrant families overcome the problems of adjusting to a new country.

Bridging the Gap

A bridge connects two separate places to each other. Young people everywhere are a kind of bridge, too. They connect the older generation to the younger generation.

As a member of your family who can speak English, you act as a kind of bridge. You're the connection from your parents' ways and language to your new country's ways and language.

Some parents may respect you for your ability to communicate in two languages, but others may feel threatened. You are still their child, yet you have become more important, more powerful. Your parents may not like the idea of being so dependent on you. They may believe that it is the parents' responsibility to advise and direct the family.

To help your parents function in an English-speaking country or try to learn English, you need to be strong, dependable, and supportive. You need to show respect for your parents and your heritage and to be sensitive to their needs. They may feel somewhat out of touch and out of control. But remember, it took an enormous amount of courage for your parents to come to a new country in the first place.

Teachers understand what it takes to master a new language.

Chapter 5

Learning English...Easy as A B C?

Have you ever watched a very young baby? Babies are usually fascinated by the sound of their own voice. If you listen carefully, you may discover that babies make many sounds that are really the beginnings of every language spoken in the world. They may make a sound that seems as if they are speaking Chinese. Or they will make a sound that is just like a word in French, Spanish, English, Russian, or Japanese. Babies are getting ready to speak. As babies grow, they are constantly hearing the sounds of their native language. They repeat the sounds that the grown-ups around them use. This is how we all learn our native language. Gradually, babies, as well as adults, forget the sounds of languages that are not repeated.

39

Forming Speech

All spoken language requires the use of voice, tongue, lips, and teeth. Using these four things in different combinations is how sounds are made.

Listen to the language your parents speak. Are there similar sounds in English? If so, it may be easier for your parents to learn English. On the other hand, if the sounds are almost totally different, then your parents have a much harder job. Your parents not only have to learn different words, but they have to change the way they position their lips, tongue, and teeth to make the sounds used in the English language.

Listen to the Beat

All languages have a beat or rhythm. Some languages have a kind of "sing-song" sound pattern. Others make abrupt starts and stops that are somewhat sharper to the ear. This is also true of individual words. The beat in each word is called a *syllable*. A word can have one beat or syllable, like car, bell, or milk. When a word has more than one syllable, like table or carrot, it is important to know where the stronger beat or *accent* should go.

A person may be familiar with a word, but if he or she doesn't stress the right syllable, the word is mispronounced. This happened to Kim's dad in the hardware store. Even though he knew the English words for the tools he wanted, he could not make himself understood.

On the Road to Learning English

Sounds? Syllables? Accent? Vocabulary? Your parents will go through a complicated process to learn English. You can be supportive and encourage their efforts. But it is also important to be patient with them.

"Teachers have long recognized that the young learn new language faster than the old. That puts you at an advantage over your parents," says Moira Reynolds in her book *Immigrant Parent*. "Then too," she continues, "it is likely that you are more exposed to the new language and therefore have a better opportunity to become proficient in it."

If you truly want your parents to learn English, explain to them why it is important. Give logical reasons that may make *them* want to learn.

Since English is the official language of the country where you and your parents live, let them know the benefits of learning English:

- They may feel that they belong.
- They can get better jobs.
- The can become more self-sufficient and less dependent on others.
- They can communicate with more people.
- They will have more control over their own lives and make more of their own decisions.

English is also considered a universal language. At home or around the world, therefore, speaking English gives you and your parents an advantage.

Word games can be fun, and can help to increase English vocabulary.

Chapter 6

How You Can Help Your Parent(s) to Learn English

There are many ways and many teaching tools in everyday life that you may be able to use to help your parents learn to speak English. You can make every time that you and your parents are together into a learning experience.

Plain Talk

In the beginning, all your conversations with your parents in English should be kept simple. At home, in a store, riding in a car or on a bus, you can identify persons, places, and things in your parents' native language. Then you can say the English word that means the same thing and ask your parents to repeat the sound. It may be helpful to begin with something your non-English-speaking parents know well.

Tanya chose to speak English to her mother while they shopped for food. Tanya spoke the English names for the products her mother put in the cart. Later that evening, when Tanya was helping her mother prepare dinner, Tanya's mother tried to repeat the correct English words for each item. She got 6 out of 10 right. Tanya gave her mother a hug.

The Radio

Ask your parents to listen to the radio. They will not be able to understand the words at first. But they will be training their ears to hear the sounds commonly used in English.

If it is possible, try to listen to the radio with your parents. Maybe they can try repeating words and phrases that they hear most often. At this point it doesn't matter what is being said—song titles, weather reports, or advertising slogans—it's all good for practice.

Kim knew that his father had little time in the day or evening to sit and talk to him. So Kim saved up to buy an inexpensive portable radio with headphones for his dad.

Kim's dad enjoyed having something to listen to while he washed dishes at work. He came over to Kim one Sunday and said loudly in clear, correctly pronounced English, "hammer," "wrench," "screwdriver." They laughed. Kim asked his father how he learned, and he pointed to his radio.

The Television

It is a good idea to watch at least one television show regularly with your parents. A situation comedy may be best. Unlike the radio that gives only the sounds, the television gives your parents the commonly used English words and expressions as well as the moving pictures that help to explain the action.

Even commercials can be used for instruction. When a commercial comes on, ask your parents what they think is happening. See how much they

Listening to tapes while doing chores is a good way to practice the unfamiliar sounds of English.

understand. You can explain anything that your parents may have missed. Because they are repeated so often, commercials may help to build vocabulary.

Some cable stations provide shows in other languages besides English. Your parents may enjoy something familiar. But also look for educational programs that are designed to teach English to non-English-speaking adults. Check the newspaper or a program listing guide. Your parents may be more comfortable and willing to work on their English in the privacy of their own home.

Books

Read aloud in English to your parents. Perhaps one of your own school books would be a good choice. If you do, three good things happen:
- Your parents hear the language.
- Your parents are learning what you are learning.
- Your parents have an opportunity to see English words in print as the words are being pronounced.

Playing Games

Try making up some simple word games to encourage your parents to speak English at home. Repeating directions and taking turns while playing a board game is another opportunity for them to practice English.

Outside Help

Tanya read an essay in the newspaper. It was about an immigrant girl who felt frustrated learning English. It was the girl's mother who suggested that they learn English together by studying five English words a day. The article gave Tanya an idea. She would teach her mother five English words a day. At least it was a start. With practice, the new vocabulary would become familiar. She went to the library and took out some books with Russian on one page and English on the facing page. While she was there, Tanya saw a big poster advertising a free library program with trained volunteers who teach English. Tanya ran all the way home. She could hardly wait to tell her mother about the free tutoring. Later she also told her about the story she had read.

While at work one day, a new restaurant employee started speaking Korean to Kim's dad. The man was obviously American. Kim's dad couldn't believe what he was hearing. "How did you learn my language?" he asked the man in his native tongue. He told Kim's dad that he was in the army stationed in Korea for several years. "When I live in a place," he said, "I like to learn the language." Kim's dad was impressed and proud. He was also inspired. If this American man had the desire to learn Korean, Kim's dad decided that he would try to learn more English. Kim's dad asked his new friend to speak to him in English from then on.

Pursuing hobbies and enjoyable activities will help to build confidence.

Chapter 7

Helping Yourself

There is a common expression: You can lead a horse to water but you can't make it drink. That means people can't be forced to do things that they don't want to do.

This may apply to your parents. Even though you think it would be in your parents' best interest to learn English, what if they don't want to? They prefer speaking in their native language. Maybe they started to learn English at one time and gave up. Or maybe they have refused to try, assuming that it would be too difficult. Some people are so afraid of failing at something new that they prefer to stay with what they already know.

Accepting What You Cannot Change

Your parents' decision not to learn English may be a great disappointment to you. You believe that they will miss out on many things in their lives and probably in yours. It may make you feel sad and angry at the same time. You will have to rethink how you can continue to be helpful to your parents knowing that they will always be somewhat dependent on you. At the same time, you must be sure to sort out your own feelings, deal with the added responsibilities, and make yourself happy.

You may need to find someone to talk to about your feelings. A social worker or counselor may help you to see that *your* life is not ruined. You can be happy, and so can your parents.

Take some time to think about the good things your parents have to offer. Are they hard-working? Loving? Supportive? Brave? Do you respect them for relocating in a new country and providing their children with opportunities for advancement? Or do you consider them to be a burden? Examine how you are judging your parents. Can you accept them for who they are?

Let's see how Tanya, Kim, Hwong, and Juan have made out.

Tanya was proud of her mother's determination to learn English and she wanted to encourage her. Tanya, however, was not willing to spend every afternoon with her mother practicing English. She wanted to be with her friends, too. She thought about her problem for a long time.

Tanya knew her mother liked to sew and crochet. She heard about a craft class that was held twice a week at the YWCA (Young Women's Christian Association). She told her mother about the class and went with her to sign her up.

Tanya's plan was working. In a couple of weeks Tanya's mother was enjoying her needlework and making new English-speaking friends. Tanya had more time to be with her friends, and her mother still was able to practice her English.

Kim's dad started spending all his free time with his new friend from work. Kim felt left out, but he didn't have the heart to tell his dad. He also didn't want to interfere with his father's progress in learning to speak English. Kim came up with an idea. He asked his dad to invite his new friend home for dinner. The evening was a success. The three of them got along very well. When the new friend from work discovered that Kim and his dad had an interest in woodworking, they all made plans to do a small construction project together. It was the beginning of many fun times that they would share.

Hwong was never able to persuade her mother to take a job at her school. Neither would her mother volunteer to plant the school garden as Hwong had hoped. No matter how hard she tried, Hwong could

Older immigrants may enjoy the company of those who
speak their native language.

*not bring her mother out of her sadness and into an
English-speaking world. Hwong's teacher finally
suggested that Hwong have a talk with the school
psychologist. Hwong didn't want to at first. She was
not used to talking about family matters with a*

stranger. But she said she would think about it if she didn't feel better soon.

In the meantime, Hwong saw a notice on the school bulletin board about meeting a pen pal. Her teacher agreed to get Hwong more information. In a few days, Hwong had the name and address of an immigrant family who had a girl Hwong's age. They had been living in Canada for only nine months. Hwong thanked her teacher. She could hardly wait for the school bell to ring so she could go home and write her first letter to her new pen pal.

Juan accepted the fact that his mother had little use for English. She seemed quite happy the way she was. Juan knew that he could not change his mother's mind. But he also knew she could not fully share in his school life or his social life. Juan decided that he would tell his mother as much as he could about school, but he would not invite her to attend meetings or activities that required him to translate. She never questioned him about it; somehow she seemed to understand.

For the most part the arrangement between Juan and his mother was working. Once when Juan had the lead in the school play, it made him sad to think that his mother could not appreciate fully how well he said his funny lines. But after the play, as the family celebrated his efforts, it didn't really seem to matter. Juan felt proud and happy in the company of his family, and most of all—loved.

Lessen the Stress

As we mentioned in Chapter 2, it is not surprising that a young person living with parents who do not speak English is often under a lot of strain. It's not easy being an adolescent and being expected to act like an adult. In time you will probably be able to manage both roles. But remember to be good to yourself along the way.

Relax. When you feel yourself getting uptight, take long, steady, deep breaths. Try to breathe more slowly. Do some stretching movements. Listen to restful music, or curl up with a good book.

Keep active. Find some time for regular exercise—walking, running, biking, tennis, or swimming—whatever you enjoy doing. Make time to be with friends.

Work on self-esteem. Keep a running list of things that you like about yourself. Praise yourself for the things that you do well.

Forgive yourself. Expect that you will make mistakes and lose your temper sometimes. It's okay. Remember that you are human. Learn from your mistakes.

Talk about it. Tell someone when you are feeling overwhelmed. There may be other family members or friends of the family who understand what you are going through. If you think you need the advice and counseling of a professional, that is available, too. (See the *Where to Get Help* section in the back of this book.)

An active social life provides an opportunity to have fun and take a
break from the responsibilities at home.

Moving On

It may help to remember that you are not alone in your situation. Like you, there are many thousands of immigrant children who speak English and grow up helping their parents to communicate and function in a new country. Whether the parents speak a little English or none at all, these children seem to understand their parents and accept the adult responsibility placed on them. And you can learn to cope with the same demands, too. By reading this book, you already have begun to try.

Adopting a positive attitude—finding something good about the situation—is always helpful. Ask yourself what advantages there are for a young person who can handle responsibility, gather information, learn new skills, and communicate in two languages! If this describes you, it sounds as if you are well on your way to becoming a capable, informed, and successful adult. Isn't that a worthwhile goal for you? Isn't that what most parents hope their children will become? Maybe you have been given a better opportunity than you realized. Try not to get too discouraged now. Maybe someday you will feel that it was well worth all your efforts.

Glossary—*Explaining New Words*

accent Speech with a foreign rhythm and pronunciation.

citizen Member of a state or nation who is guaranteed certain rights and accepts certain responsibilities.

communicate To give or exchange information.

generation All the people born or living at about the same time.

heritage The history, culture, and tradition passed on to a later generation.

idiom An expression or group of words that have a special meaning.

immigrants People who leave the country in which they were born to live in another country for good. They are granted legal permanent residence.

"melting pot" The idea that many different races would come together and be transformed into a new people.

multicultural Having to do with the ideas, arts, customs, skills, etc. of several different groups of people.

native language The language a person first learns. It is usually the language of the country where he or she was born.

refugees People who have come to another country to live for an extended time because it is not safe for them to stay in the country where they were born.

sound pattern A group of sounds that the human speech organs can utter.

stress Feeling of pressure or strain; anxiety.

syllable A unit of one or more sounds within a word.

trait A recognized quality in a person.

translate To put into the words of a different language.

vocabulary All the words recognized and understood by a particular person.

Where to Get Help

There are many outside sources that teach English. Many of these are free. It could be an organized program of trained volunteers, or simply one person helping another. Check out some of the following places in your local area.

- *Public Libraries*. May sponsor volunteer programs for learning English or have information available on other local programs. Also a valuable resource for reference books that explain things like filling out forms, getting a social security card, or becoming a citizen.
- *Adult Education Courses*. Call the public schools in your area for information.
- *Religious organizations*.
- *Community centers*.
- *National organizations*. Some may offer language courses locally. Look in your telephone book for:

YMCA (Young Men's Christian Association)
YWCA (Young Women's Christian Association)
YMHA (Young Men's Hebrew Association)

Having a pen pal may offer you friendship and a chance to practice English. Contact any of the following:

International Pen Friends
P.O. Box 290065
Brooklyn, NY 11229   (718) 769-1785

Worldwide Friendship International
3749 Brice Run Road, Suite A
Randallstown, MD 21133   (301) 922-2795

Student Letter Exchange
630 Third Avenue
New York, N.Y. 10017   (212) 557-3312

• *Other family services in the United States:*

American Red Cross
United Way
Catholic Social Services

American Refugee Commission
2344 Nicollet Avenue
Minneapolis, MN 55404

Lutheran Immigration and Refugee Service
390 Park Avenue South
New York, NY 10016

National Center for Urban Ethnic Affairs (NCUEA)
P.O. Box 20, Cardinal Station
Washington, DC 20064

National Coalition of Advocates for Students
100 Boylston Street
Boston, MA 02116-4610

New York Association for New Americans
730 Broadway
New York, NY 10003

Puerto Rican Family Institute
116 West 114th Street
New York, NY 10025

• *Canadian agencies for family services:*

**Affiliation of Multicultural Societies and
    Services of British Columbia**
1254 West 7th Avenue
Vancouver, BC V6H 186

**Association of Parent Support Groups in
    Ontario**
11 Nevada Avenue
Willowdale, ON M2M 3N9

**Canadian Association of Neighbourhood
    Services (CANS)**
3102 Main Street
Vancouver, BC V5T 3G7

Canadian Institute on Minority Rights
4404 St. Dominique
Montreal, PQ H2G 3CB

Family Service Canada
Jewish Immigrant Aid Service of Canada
4600 Bathurst Street
Willowdale, ON M2R 3V3

Ontario Council of Agencies Serving Immigrants
579 St. Clair Avenue
West Toronto, ON M6C 1A3

For Further Reading

Ashabranner, Brent. *The New Americans.* New York: Dodd, Mead and Co., 1983.

Bode, Janet. *New Kids on the Block.* New York: Franklin Watts, 1989.

Morey, Janet N., and Dunn, Wendy. *Famous Asian Americans.* Cobblehill Books, 1989.

Reimers, David M. *The Immigrant Experience.* New York: Chelsea House Publishers, 1989.

Reynolds, Moira Davison. *Coping with an Immigrant Parent.* New York: The Rosen Publishing Group, 1993.

Stanek, Muriel. *I Speak English for My Mom.* Chicago: Albert Whitman, 1989.

Index

About the Author
Patricia Lakin is a first-generation American on her mother's side. For the past fifteen years, she has been writing fiction and nonfiction for children. Ms. Lakin is married and is the mother of two boys. She and her family live in New York City. For her, the wealth of accents, languages, and customs is one of the city's major attractions.

Photo Credits
Cover Photo by Stuart Rabinowitz.
Photos on pages 2, 8, 13, 36, 38, 52: AP/Wide World; page 17: © Carolyn Gangi/Gamma Liaison; pages 20, 27, 30, 32, 42, 45, 48, 55: Stuart Rabinowitz; page 24: © Anthony Suau/Gamma Liaison.

Design/Production: Blackbirch Graphics, Inc.